Poems for Your Pocket

Poetry to Keep with You

Compiled and Illustrated
by Grace Russo

ISBN 979-8-9929772-4-0

Illustrations were created on Legion Stonehenge Paper
with Micron Pens.
Typeset in Span Condensed.

This edition published by Pennyworth Publishing
in 2026.

Visit us at PennyworthPub.com

Table of Contents

Table of Contents

Foreword

Poetry memorization is not so popular as it once was, but vestiges live on. Songs and jingles get stuck in our heads. Funny posts, memes, and all manner of viral emphemera live on in our minds long after the websites have gone defunct or been abandoned by most of their users. We have not lost the ability, then, to memorize. Let this little book be your motivation to start tucking away lines of verse, just for yourself, in your own head. It is one of the only places you can keep things for free, after all. The poems advance in length as the book progresses, but feel free to begin wherever you please—as long as you begin.

A Flower Given To My Daughter

BY JAMES JOYCE

Frail the white rose and frail are
Her hands that gave
Whose soul is sere and paler
Than time's wan wave.

Rosefrail and fair—yet frailest
A wonder wild
In gentle eyes thou veilest,
My blueveined child.

(1913)

Canis Major

ROBERT FROST

The great Overdog
That heavenly beast
With a star in one eye
Gives a leap in the east.
He dances upright
All the way to the west
And never once drops
On his forefeet to rest.
I'm a poor underdog,
But to-night I will bark
With the great Overdog
That romps through the dark.

(1928)

A Burnt Ship

JOHN DONNE

Out of a fired ship, which by no way
But drowning could be rescued from the flame,
Some men leap'd forth, and ever as they came
Near the foes' ships, did by their shot decay;
So all were lost, which in the ship were found,
    They in the sea being burnt, they in
        the burnt ship drown'd.

(1623)

The Woodpecker

ELIZABETH MADOX ROBERTS

The woodpecker pecked out a little round hole
And made him a house in the telephone pole.
One day when I watched he poked out his head,
And he had on a hood and a collar of red.
When the streams of rain pour out of the sky,
And the sparkles of lightning go flashing by,
And the big, big wheels of thunder roll,
He can snuggle back in the telephone pole.

(1930)

The Dawn

I would be as ignorant as the dawn,
That has looked down
On that old queen measuring a town
With the pin of a brooch,
Or on the withered men that saw
From their pedantic Babylon
The careless planets in their courses,
The stars fade out where the moon comes,
And took their tablets and made sums–
Yet did but look, rocking the glittering coach
Above the cloudy shoulders of the horses.
I would be–for no knowledge is worth a straw–
Ignorant and wanton as the dawn.

(1917)

9

Loveliest of Trees, the Cherry Now

A. E. HOUSMAN

Loveliest of trees, the cherry now
Is hung with bloom along the bough,
And stands about the woodland ride
Wearing white for Eastertide.
Now, of my threescore years and ten,
Twenty will not come again,
And take from seventy springs a score,
It only leaves me fifty more.
And since to look at things in bloom
Fifty springs are little room,
About the woodlands I will go
To see the cherry hung with snow.

(1895)

Thrushes

SIEGFRIED SASSOON

Tossed on the glittering air they soar and skim,
Whose voices make the emptiness of light
A windy palace. Quavering from the brim
Of dawn, and bold with song at edge of night,
They clutch their leafy pinnacles and sing
Scornful of man, and from his toils aloof
Whose heart's a haunted woodland whispering;
Whose thoughts return on tempest-baffledwing;
Who hears the cry of God in everything,
And storms the gate of nothingness for proof.

(1918)

13

Water Lilies

A. A. MILNE

Where the water-lilies go
To and fro,
Rocking in the ripples of the water,
Lazy on a leaf lies the Lake King's daughter,
And the faint winds shake her.
Who will come and take her?
I will! I will!
Keep still! Keep still!

Sleeping on a leaf lies the Lake King's
                    daughter...
Then the wind comes skipping
To the lilies on the water;
And the kind winds wake her.
Now who will take her?
With a laugh she is slipping
Through the lilies on the water.

Wait! Wait!
Too late, too late!
Only the water-lilies go
To and fro,
Dipping, dipping,
To the ripples of the water.

(1925)

A Study (A Soul)

CHRISTINA ROSSETTI

She stands as pale as Parian statues stand;
Like Cleopatra when she turned at bay,
And felt her strength above the Roman sway,
And felt the aspic writhing in her hand.
Her face is steadfast toward the shadowy land,
For dim beyond it looms the light of day;
Her feet are steadfast; all the arduous way
That foot-track hath not wavered on the sand.
She stands there like a beacon thro' the night,
A pale clear beacon where the storm-drift is;
She stands alone, a wonder deathly white;
She stands there patient, nerved with inner might,
Indomitable in her feebleness,
Her face and will athirst against the light.

(1896)

Gold Leaves

G. K. CHESTERTON

Lo! I am come to autumn,
When all the leaves are gold;
Grey hairs and golden leaves cry out
The year and I are old.

In youth I sought the prince of men,
Captain in cosmic wars,
Our Titan, even the weeds would show
Defiant, to the stars.

But now a great thing in the street
Seems any human nod,
Where shift in strange democracy
The million masks of God.

In youth I sought the golden flower
Hidden in wood or wold,
But I am come to autumn,
When all the leaves are gold.

(1900)

19

Song: My Silks and Fine Array

WILLIAM BLAKE

My silks and fine array,
    My smiles and languish'd air,
By love are driv'n away;
    And mournful lean Despair
Brings me yew to deck my grave:
Such end true lovers have.

His face is fair as heav'n,
    When springing buds unfold;
O why to him was't giv'n,
    Whose heart is wintry cold?
His breast is love's all worship'd tomb,
Where all love's pilgrims come.

Bring me an axe and spade,
    Bring me a winding sheet;

When I my grave have made,
    Let winds and tempests beat:
Then down I'll lie, as cold as clay.
True love doth pass away!

(1783)

The Mushroom

EMILY DICKINSON

The mushroom is the elf of plants,
At evening it is not;
At morning in a truffled hut
It stops upon a spot

As if it tarried always;
And yet its whole career
Is shorter than a snake's delay,
And fleeter than a tare.

'T is vegetation's juggler,
The germ of alibi;
Doth like a bubble antedate,
And like a bubble hie.

I feel as if the grass were pleased
To have it intermit;

The surreptitious scion
Of summer's circumspect.

Had nature any outcast face,
Could she a son contemn,
Had nature an Iscariot,
That mushroom, it is him.

(1891)

Invictus

WILLIAM ERNEST HENLEY

Out of the night that covers me,
  Black as the pit from pole to pole,
I thank whatever gods may be
  For my unconquerable soul.

In the fell clutch of circumstance
  I have not winced nor cried aloud.
Under the bludgeonings of chance
  My head is bloody, but unbowed.

Beyond this place of wrath and tears
  Looms but the Horror of the shade,
And yet the menace of the years
  Finds and shall find me unafraid.

It matters not how strait the gate,
  How charged with punishments the scroll,

I am the master of my fate,
   I am the captain of my soul.

(1888)

Ode on Solitude

ALEXANDER POPE

Happy the man, whose wish and care
  A few paternal acres bound,
Content to breathe his native air,
          In his own ground.

Whose herds with milk, whose fields with bread,
  Whose flocks supply him with attire,
Whose trees in summer yield him shade,
          In winter fire.

Blest, who can unconcernedly find
  Hours, days, and years slide soft away,
In health of body, peace of mind,
          Quiet by day,

Sound sleep by night; study and ease,
  Together mixed; sweet recreation;

And innocence, which most does please,
        With meditation.

Thus let me live, unseen, unknown;
  Thus unlamented let me die;
Steal from the world, and not a stone
        Tell where I lie.

(1726)

On the Grasshopper and the Cricket

JOHN KEATS

The Poetry of earth is never dead:
  When all the birds are faint with the hot sun,
  And hide in cooling trees, a voice will run
From hedge to hedge about the new-mown mead;
That is the Grasshopper's—he takes the lead
  In summer luxury,—he has never done
  With his delights; for when tired out with fun
He rests at ease beneath some pleasant weed.
The poetry of earth is ceasing never:
  On a lone winter evening, when the frost
  Has wrought a silence, from the stove there shrills
The Cricket's song, in warmth increasing ever,
  And seems to one in drowsiness half lost,
    The Grasshopper's among some grassy hills.

(1816)

As Kingfishers Catch Fire

GERARD MANLEY HOPKINS

As kingfishers catch fire, dragonflies draw flame;
As tumbled over rim in roundy wells
Stones ring; like each tucked string tells, each hung
bell's
Bow swung finds tongue to fling out broad its
name;
Each mortal thing does one thing and the same:
Deals out that being indoors each one dwells;
Selves—goes itself; myself it speaks and spells,
Crying Whát I dó is me: for that I came.

I say móre: the just man justices;
Keeps grace: thát keeps all his goings graces;
Acts in God's eye what in God's eye he is—
Chríst—for Christ plays in ten thousand places,

Lovely in limbs, and lovely in eyes not his
To the Father through the features of men's faces.

(1918)

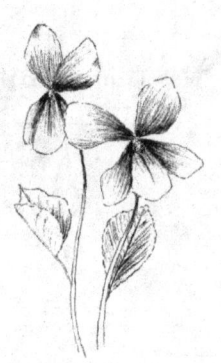

Sonnet 99

WILLIAM SHAKESPEARE

The forward violet thus did I chide:
Sweet thief, whence didst thou steal thy sweet that
smells,
If not from my love's breath? The purple pride
Which on thy soft cheek for complexion dwells
In my love's veins thou hast too grossly dyed.
The lily I condemned for thy hand,
And buds of marjoram had stol'n thy hair:
The roses fearfully on thorns did stand;
A third, nor red nor white, had stol'n of both
And to his robbery had annex'd thy breath;
But, for his theft, in pride of all his growth
A vengeful canker eat him up to death.
   More flowers I noted, yet I none could see
    But sweet or colour it had stol'n from thee.

(1609)

Change upon Change

ELIZABETH BARRETT BROWNING

Five months ago the stream did flow,
  The lilies bloomed within the sedge,
And we were lingering to and fro,
Where none will track thee in this snow,
  Along the stream, beside the hedge.
Ah, Sweet, be free to love and go!
  For if I do not hear thy foot,
  The frozen river is as mute,
  The flowers have dried down to the root:
And why, since these be changed since May,
  Shouldst thou change less than they.

And slow, slow as the winter snow
  The tears have drifted to mine eyes;
And my poor cheeks, five months ago
Set blushing at thy praises so,
  Put paleness on for a disguise.
Ah, Sweet, be free to praise and go!

For if my face is turned too pale,
It was thine oath that first did fail, –
It was thy love proved false and frail, –
And why, since these be changed enow,
   Should I change less than thou.

(1851)

Annabel Lee

EDGAR ALLAN POE

It was many and many a year ago,
  In a kingdom by the sea,
That a maiden there lived whom you may know
  By the name of Annabel Lee;
And this maiden she lived with no other thought
  Than to love and be loved by me.

I was a child and she was a child,
  In this kingdom by the sea,
But we loved with a love that was more than love—
  I and my Annabel Lee—
With a love that the wingèd seraphs of Heaven
  Coveted her and me.

And this was the reason that, long ago,
  In this kingdom by the sea,
A wind blew out of a cloud, chilling

My beautiful Annabel Lee;
So that her highborn kinsmen came
    And bore her away from me,
To shut her up in a sepulchre
    In this kingdom by the sea.

The angels, not half so happy in Heaven,
    Went envying her and me—
Yes!—that was the reason (as all men know,
    In this kingdom by the sea)
That the wind came out of the cloud by night,
    Chilling and killing my Annabel Lee

But our love it was stronger by far than the love
    Of those who were older than we—
    Of many far wiser than we—
And neither the angels in Heaven above
    Nor the demons down under the sea
Can ever dissever my soul from the soul
    Of the beautiful Annabel Lee;

For the moon never beams, without bringing me
dreams
   Of the beautiful Annabel Lee;
And the stars never rise, but I feel the bright eyes
   Of the beautiful Annabel Lee;
And so, all the night-tide, I lie down by the side
   Of my darling—my darling—my life and my bride,

   In her sepulchre there by the sea—
   In her tomb by the sounding sea.

(1849)

The Duel

EUGENE FIELD

The gingham dog and the calico cat
Side by side on the table sat;
'T was half-past twelve, and (what do you think!)
Nor one nor t' other had slept a wink!
    The old Dutch clock and the Chinese plate
    Appeared to know as sure as fate
There was going to be a terrible spat.
        (I was n't there; I simply state
        What was told to me by the Chinese plate!)

The gingham dog went "Bow-wow-wow!"
And the calico cat replied "Mee-ow!"
The air was littered, an hour or so,
With bits of gingham and calico,
    While the old Dutch clock in the
chimney-place
    Up with its hands before its face,

For it always dreaded a family row!
    (Now mind: I'm only telling you
    What the old Dutch clock declares is true!)

The Chinese plate looked very blue,
And wailed, "Oh, dear! what shall we do!"
But the gingham dog and the calico cat
Wallowed this way and tumbled that,
    Employing every tooth and claw
    In the awfullest way you ever saw—
And, oh! how the gingham and calico flew!
    (Don't fancy I exaggerate—
    I got my news from the Chinese plate!)
Next morning, where the two had sat
They found no trace of dog or cat;
And some folks think unto this day
That burglars stole that pair away!
    But the truth about the cat and pup

Is this: they ate each other up!
Now what do you really think of that!
    (The old Dutch clock it told me so,
    And that is how I came to know.)

(1892)

Original Publication Information

"A Flower Given To My Daughter" by James Joyce was written in 1913 and first published in *Pomes Penyeach* in 1927.

"Canis Major" by Robert Frost was first published in *West-Running Brook* in 1928.

"A Burnt Ship" by John Donne was first published posthumously in *Poems, by J.D. VVith Elegies on the Author's Death* in 1623.

"The Woodpecker" by Elizabeth Madox Roberts was first published in *Under the Tree* in 1922.

"The Dawn" by W. B. Yeats was first published in *The Swans at Coole* in 1916.

"Loveliest of Trees, the Cherry Now" by A. E. Houseman was originally published in *A Shropshire Lad* in 1895.

"Thrushes" by Siegfried Sassoon was originally published in *The New Statesman* in 1918.

"Water Lilies" by A. A. Milne was originally pubilshed in *When We Were Very Young* in 1925.

"A Study (A Soul)" by Christina Rossetti was written in 1854 and published posthumously in *New Poems by Christina Rossetti, hitherto unpublished or uncollected* in 1896.

"Gold Leaves" by G. K. Chesterton was originally published in *The Wild Knight & Other Poems* in 1900.

"Song: My Silks and Fine Array" by William Blake was originally published in *Poetical Sketches* in 1783.

"The Mushroom" by Emily Dickenson was originally published posthumously in *The Poems of Emily Dickenson: Series Two* in 1896.

"Invictus" by William Ernest Henley was written in 1975 and published in *Book of Verses* in 1888.

"Ode on Solitude" by Alexander Pope was written in 1700 and originally published in *Miscellaneous Poems, Translation and Immitations by Several Hands* in 1726.

"On the Grasshopper and the Cricket" by John Keats was originally published in *The Examiner* in 1816.

"As Kingfishers Catch Fire" by Gerard Manley Hopkins was written in 1877 but published posthumously in *Poems of Gerard Manley Hopkins* in 1918.

"Sonnet 99" By William Shakespeare was originally published in *Shake-speares Sonnets: Never Before Imprinted* in 1609.

"Change upon Change" by Elizabeth Barrett Browning was originally published in *Prometheus Bound, and other poems* in 1851.

"Annabel Lee" by Edgar Allan Poe was written in 1849 and published posthumously in *The Works of the Late Edgar Allan Poe, vol 2*, in 1859.

"The Duel" by Eugene Field was written after 1892 and published posthumously in *Poems That Every Child Should Know* in 1904.

About the Illustrator

Grace Russo is a wife and mother who has always enjoyed capturing facets of beauty in drawing, painting, and fiber arts. As her children grew, so did her desire to give them books which reflected the joy and beauty of creation and the intricacy of the English language. Thus was born her first book project, and, with it, Pennyworth Publishing.